SK8
ESSENTIALS

Written by Mike Saiz
Designed by the Top That! Team

Copyright © 2002 Top That! Publishing plc
Published by Tangerine Press™, an imprint of Scholastic Inc.
557 Broadway, New York, NY 10012.
All rights reserved
Scholastic and Tangerine Press and associated logos are trademarks of Scholastic Inc.
Printed and bound in China

24 Contents

Skateboarders seem to be everywhere you look: in city centers, parks, shopping malls, and in specially designed skateparks.

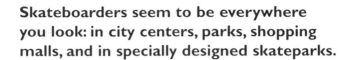

Have Fun
Whether you're just in it for fun or you want to compete, skateboarding is an enjoyable way to keep fit and have fun.

Be Safe
So what do you need to become a skateboarder? What skills must be learned, and how much will it cost? Over the course of this book, all these questions and many others will be answered. You'll discover why this exhilarating sport has so many participants from all backgrounds and age groups.

Photos are intended to demonstrate technique, not illustrate safety precautions. Be sure to wear protective gear everytime you skate.

Skating Terms
Use the glossary at the back if you want to check the meanings of any of the words used. Before you know it, you'll learn a whole new language — skater-speak.

It may seem skateboarders have been around longer than roller, or in-line, skaters, but roller skaters provided modern skateboarders with the foundations and equipment that allowed skateboarding to flourish.

In the Beginning

The invention of the wheel in prehistoric times was majorly cool because it meant the start of transport on wheels. Belgian John Joseph Merlin made the first kind of skate in the 1760s, and this spawned the roller skate.

In 1884 — now this is the big one – came the invention of the ball bearing, which meant smooth riding and fast speeds.

Forget the Handle

In the 1940s, people started taking metal skates apart and hammering the footplate parts to planks of wood. This was the start of the skateboard. In the 1950s, scooters with a T–shaped handlebar were popular. When someone broke off the handle by mistake, the skateboard was born!

Sidewalk Surfing

In 1958, A.C. Boyden (Humco) patented the earliest recognizable skateboard. Around this time, the term "sidewalk surfing" was coined by surfers, who used the board as a way of getting around and "carving" on the concrete. Even today, surf language is closely intertwined with skater-speak.

Mini Surfboards

Early skateboards resembled mini surfboards but were quite small in length and width. Made from different types of solid woods, they had narrow trucks with clay compound wheels.

Kicktails

Early skateboards had no kicktails. Invented and patented in 1967 by Larry Stevenson, kicktails enabled tighter turning, braking, and tricks. Carving and freestyle skating were popular at this point.

Skatewear

Skate clothing started to appear in the 1970s. Vans was the first skate shoe company.

'70s Skating

In the 1970s, urethane wheels and precision bearings were introduced, giving superior grip and ride quality. In the mid- to late 1970s, techniques such as pool riding, vert, freestyle, slalom, and pipe riding were introduced. Also, different types of boards and wheels were developed.

Popular Stuff

Skateboarding's popularity began to grow wildly toward the end of the 1990s. Today, it's big business, and millions of skaters worldwide enjoy a sport that has its own heroes, TV programs, music, clothing, and language.

Let's take a closer look at the skateboard. There are actually very few parts to something that will have you bustin' air and grinding till the sun goes down.

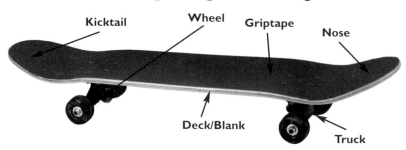

Kicktail Wheel Griptape Nose

Deck/Blank Truck

Deck or Blank

Usually laminated maple, most modern decks have a double kick and are slightly concave, giving a surer feel when sessioning.

Wheelbase

The wheelbase (the distance between the trucks) changes a board's feel. A shorter wheelbase, less than 13 inches (33 cm), is good for spins and turns.

A wheelbase of more than 15 inches (38 cm) feels more stable but is harder to turn. The secret is to go for a 14-inch (35-cm) wheelbase.

Board Width

Today, most boards are around 32 inches (81 cm) long, 8 inches (20 cm) wide. The wider the board, the more stable it is, but it becomes harder to flip.

Kicktail & Composition

Most decks have a double kicktail, used to do tricks and keep feet anchored. The composition of most boards today is seven-ply maple laminate. This can crack or delaminate, but it is generally pretty rigid and great for tricks.

Griptape

Griptape is a textured material on the top of the deck to help you stay put when boarding.

Wheels

Wheels are usually around 2 inches (5 cm) in diameter. Check the durometer scale below to know what to look for when choosing a pair. Remember: Big wheels of 3 inches (7 cm) are fast, soft wheels are slow, small wheels (1.5 inches [3.5 cm]) mean a bumpy ride, and big wheels mean a smooth ride. That said,

small wheels accelerate more quickly but lose speed more quickly. The best ones all-around are 2.5 inches (6 cm) and medium-hard, or 95A on the scale.

Trucks

These beauties, mostly made from aluminium or alloy mixes, are suspension and steering units, held to the deck by the baseplate and locking bolts. Wheels are attached to an axle that runs through the hanger (the bit you grind on). This is

secured to the baseplate with the kingpin. Threaded onto this are two bushings (like doughnuts), which soften steering and return the truck to the neutral position.

Flipping and Spinning

Trucks on new boards should be no wider than the board. Slightly narrower ones aid flipping and spinning the board.

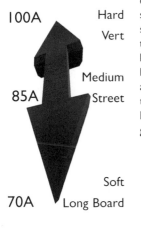

100A   Hard

Vert

Medium

85A   Street

Soft

70A   Long Board

Truck

Wheel

Old-style '70s wheels and trucks

7

Follow the tips here, and you'll be skating safely as well as in style.

Sites
Never skate in traffic, on private property, in the dark, on gravel, in wet conditions, alone, or when people don't know where you are or where you're going.

Safety Gear
A little extra help with protective clothing is a good idea. You may see lots of skaters tearing up the ramps, boxes, and streets without proper safety clothing. Do not attempt to copy them! Skating can be dangerous, and without the proper safety equipment you may become injured and unable to do the sport that you love.

Get Kitted Out
Watch the pro skaters in competition. They have all the moves. Why are they so good? One reason is that if they wipe out, they get up and try again. They didn't get that cool by having their legs, arms, and wrists in plaster, unable to skate for weeks. So, to give yourself a confident and relatively painless start, slap on some pads and a helmet. You will find your learning curve greatly improves if you do not fear hurting yourself when you fall over!

Armor
So after all this, what should you wear?

• **Wrist guards** — These are plastic splints that support the — you guessed it — wrist.

Most skate injuries are to the wrist, so don't go skating without them.

• **Elbow pads** — These Velcro pads fasten above and below the elbow. They have a hardened outer pad for extra protection on impact and are absolutely essential for beginners.

• **Kneepads** — These are similar to elbow pads. Some have extra protection on the sides

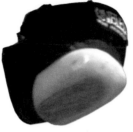

of the knee. They are crucial for vertical riding and for a safe escape from failed tricks.

• **Helmet (Lid)** — The helmet protects the head. Make sure it fits well and comes down far enough to protect the back of the head. You may never hit your head — statistically it is one of the least likely body parts to be hurt — but it contains your brain, so look after it.

• **Clothes** — Always wear clothes that will perform and protect for the sport you choose. Loose, hard-wearing clothing is best. Skate shoes are designed to give you maximum grip, so don't think of wearing running shoes or anything with a heel.

Pro Tip

Spend as much as you can on your board and skating clothes. Good equipment will help you to learn faster and will make you look the part!

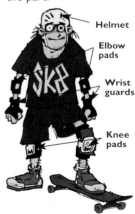

Helmet
Elbow pads
Wrist guards
Knee pads

Let's be honest here: You will fall at some point, get bruised, and maybe bleed a bit, but hey — if it were that easy, we would have wheels, not feet!

Stretch and Lift

Warming up and stretching could make all the difference between landing that wild 180-degree ollie or being laid up with an ice pack on your knee after a bad 50–50. Before you go out, stretch your legs, back, and sides, do a few leg pulls, and climb some stairs.

Water, Water

Always carry water. Not only will it quench your thirst but if you get a scrape, a quick splash of water will clean it until more effective measures can be taken. If you are badly cut, black out, or you are seeing stars, seek immediate medical attention.

Warm up Style

Go through a few easy tricks just to get your mind and body ready. If you don't warm up, your first drop into the vert may be the last for that session.

Pro Tip

Keep your weight forward when skating. The worst injuries you will get when learning will be when you flip off the back of your deck. When this happens, you have very little way of stopping yourself because your arms simply don't bend this way! If you feel yourself doing this, twist around so you can see what you're going to hit. This way, you can anticipate the impact and brace yourself.

Buying Your First Board

By the time you go to buy your first board, you probably will have borrowed someone else's and gotten the fever. But how do you know which boards are the best? Simple: Just read this guide.

Do Not ...

buy from department stores because generally they carry a limited range. Besides, most of these stores carry toys. You do not want a toy. You need performance, grip, and strength, so that when you start to do tricks, your board won't break, and your trucks will stay on.

Do ...

buy from skate shops where the owners will have more knowledge and a wider selection of skateboards to help you make the right decision. They may even help you to assemble the board if you don't have the tools at home.

Checklist

When buying a first board, most people opt for one that is already assembled. This should have a good deck, a solid truck system, decent bearings, a smooth ride and good wheels (2.5-inch [6-cm] diameter with medium-hard wheels). It should also be at least ABC5. Check the ABC ratings on the bearings. Usually, the higher the number, the better. Look for ABC5 or ABC7. Make sure the wheels are the right size and hardness for the type of skating you are going to do. You need small, hard wheels for aggressive skating and big, soft wheels for land cruising and downhill skating.

Buying Armor

Buy armor at the same time as you buy your skates. When you fall the first few times, you will be grateful for the protection. You may even be able to get a good discount if you buy your board and safety equipment at the same time.

TOP TIP
Buy before the weather gets warm. Prices rise with the heat.

OK, you have the armor and the deck of your dreams, and you're ready to start. A skatepark may seem like the coolest place to start skating, but in fact it's perhaps the worst place to learn. You could end up hurt or causing someone else to get hurt trying to avoid you.

Learn the Basics

To a novice, the way skaters leap onto rails, catch air, and flip their boards may seem impossible to master, but with a lot of practice, you will soon be in the thick of the action. Remember, practice makes perfect, and time spent now will save you a lot of cuts and bruises in the future. Go to a park or relatively quiet place with a gentle hill, such as a closed parking lot, and you can start to learn the basics. When you get on your board, do it naturally.

Natural or Goofy

If your left foot is at the front, you are natural, if your right is at the front you are goofy. (Don't worry; goofy is just a term!) Put whichever foot you favor on the deck, gently push off with the other, and step fully onto the deck. Then roll.

Moving Off

If you are going too slowly, push a few more times. Roll your heels back while moving. The deck will move, and you will turn. Push the balls of your feet in and — presto — you turn the other way. Practice this, and as you get more confident, carve out some tighter turns.

Emergency Stop

If you need to stop, you can do one of two things:

A. Take your pushing foot off your deck and place it on the ground, as if you're going to take a step. But instead of pushing, use the impact to reduce your speed. You may have to do this a few times to slow down.

B. If you are going quite fast, jump off your deck and run alongside till you can stop.

Power Slides and Wheelies

Some other ways of stopping are the power slide and a tail manual (wheelie). These are worth mentioning because they are fun!

The power slide, shown in the pictures on this page, involves deciding when you want to stop, going into a very tight turn and at the same time, and planting your hand down.

You use your hand to push your board around and slow down. This kind of move is also used on mellow bowls and ramps. An extension of this move is a handplant on a rail.

Another way of stopping is to go into a tail manual and carve a tight turn. As you are doing this, drag your tail foot's toe on the ground.

Skate Stance

The way you stand on your deck, whether it's natural or goofy, makes little difference in the level of tricks you can do, so don't feel like you have to change your stance if you are the only goofy-footed member of your crew. Similarly, it doesn't matter if you push with your deck foot at the front or back of the board. The most important thing to remember is to do what feels best for you and stick to it. Only you can decide the best way for you to skate.

Switch Stance

However, there is always an exception to the rule and this is one of them. Being able to skate "switch stance" (the opposite to your usual stance) can help you land and execute some tricks that involve entering or leaving in a switch stance. When you can switch stance,

it will greatly improve your tricktionary. Being able to skate "fakie" (backward) with ease will also help you to be comfortable with entering or exiting a trick, whether it's street or vert.

Trick Shot

So now that you know the basic maneuvers, do you feel ready to learn some tricks? A lot of tricks seem to defy gravity, and it may be difficult to break down exactly what's happening, no matter how many times you watch a trick. This is partly because of the speed at which they are happening, but you need to know where to look for the vital clues.

Trick Terminology

A lot of tricks rely on specific foot position

and the distribution of weight. Without knowing this, most tricks would be impossible. Being comfortable on your deck and being able to feel the way it moves under you will help you understand what follows. So when you read words such as "pressure" and "feel," relate them to your feet and deck. Use the glossary at the back for any words that you don't understand.

This trick isn't really a trick at all but more of a way of turning and moving without taking your feet off the deck. It seems simple, but it will give you your first chance to feel the effect of shifting your weight.

Technique

To tick-tack, raise the nose of your deck and move it from side to side, momentarily touching the ground on the end of each arc. To do this, apply pressure to the back kicktail by shifting your weight back and positioning your back foot over the kicktail. Each time that your front wheels leave the ground, you are pulling a nose manual.

1. Notice the position of the front foot. It needs to be roughly on top of the front truck or slightly behind, so that more weight is at the back of the deck.

2. Apply slight pressure to the kick to get the nose in the air.

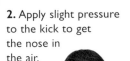

3. Move the nose either left or right before bringing it down to the ground. Repeat this movement in the opposite direction. Continue to do this to produce momentum and speed.

Moonwalking
Once you have mastered this basic technique, you could try a move called moonwalking. This is like tick-tacking, but you do not place your nose down after each arc. Instead, you swing your nose from side to side. If nothing else, it's a good balancing exercise. Getting the feel of tick-tacking and moonwalking will help you to learn the manual (wheelie). The manual involves raising the nose of your board and holding it there. Landing a trick while doing a manual is always an impressive move. Once you can do this well, practice a nose manual to give you an edge for when you try balancing nose grinds later in the book.

First invented in 1978 by a skater called Alan 'Ollie' Gelfand (although another claimant is Rodney Mullen), this is, without doubt, the most important trick in skateboard history. Without it, the sport would have remained in the Dark Ages.

For Starters

The ollie starts off many complex tricks. Mastering both nose and tail ollies will catapult you into trick nirvana.

Technique

This is the basic ollie technique; super air ollies will only come with practice. Try to learn it while moving, as you rarely do an ollie while stationary.

1. Start by riding forward, rear foot on the tail, front foot halfway down. The weight should be on the balls of your feet. See photos 1A and 1B for foot position and stance.

1A

1B

2. Pay attention: This is the tricky part. A lot of weight shifting is involved here, and timing is critical. Start by stamping on the tail. As you jump into the air, your front foot must stay in very light contact with the deck. At the very same time as this jump action, your board will jump. For a good test of the action, get off your board and stamp on the tail. It will jump into the air. Now imagine your front foot holding the nose down a bit.

3. When you are catching air, drag your front foot toward the nose to level the board out. Both legs should be bent underneath you, and the deck should be flat underneath you at the end of this part of the ollie trick.

4. If all has gone to plan, gravity will pull you down. Keep your legs bent and prepare to land. Now you can ollie to your heart's content!

Pro Tip

If you can't do this trick while moving, try it while stationary on some carpet. The mechanics are the same, but there is no hazardous concrete!

You've mastered the ollie; now try a frontside 180-degree ollie.

Technique 1–2. Start the trick the same as with the ollie, but with the front foot three-quarters of the way up the deck, rear foot central on the tail.

3. As you pop it, drag your back foot around and your front foot in the opposite direction.

4–5. As you do this, spin in midair and land fakie. Do not try to move the deck the whole way with one foot. You have to move the deck around with both feet. Practice this, then try a backside version.

With most tricks, it's best to learn frontside and backside versions. If you do not commit fully to this trick, you will still land and live to tell the tale – so really go for it.

Grinding? Do a 50–50

Always approach grinds with speed and attitude. Remember your trucks are metal, and they need momentum to slide along rails and ledges. Once again, this trick starts with the ollie to launch you onto the rail or curb.

1. To start with, approach the object you are going to grind at about 30 degrees. Upon mastery, you can approach it as you like.

2. Ollie up and push your trailing foot out so that your back truck lands on the edge first.

Technique

As the name suggests, you are going to grind the trucks equally, back and front, 50–50. To do this, you will need nerves of steel. Do not try this for the first time on a rail or you may hurt yourself. This first grind is similar to doing the grind on a rail. Try it this way first to lesson the chance of it going wrong. Go in fast, and don't lose your nerve as you approach.

3. As soon as this happens, move your weight forward and get the front truck down and grinding. In this position, you should be grinding along nicely with your wheels keeping you nice and stable.

4. In this position, grind until you start to stall or need to exit the trick. To do this, put your weight toward the back, kick off, and there you have it. As with all tricks, it can be done frontside, backside,

fakie, or regular. For added fun, you could land it on the nose or just the tail. This takes a lot more balance, and you have to be competent at tail and nose manuals before even thinking about trying it, or you will risk getting hurt.

The noseslide is a very versatile trick. It can be done on low curbs or high stair rails. Obviously, to get to higher rails, an ollie or ramp must be used. This trick can also be used on the vert as a way to use the coping and move along the ramp.

1. Approach the curb at a shallow angle. As with most approaches, it's best to start at around 30 to 45 degrees. Note the position of the feet in this trick. You will be shifting your weight backward and forward.

The Object

The aim is to land the nose on the kerb. You need to hit the curb at speed — the more speed, the longer the slides. Too little speed will grab your board and throw you.

Technique

First, pick a good clean curb. Some people wax the curb with paraffin or candles to aid sliding.

2. As you approach the curb, raise the nose of the board. As the nose of the board goes over the curb, shift all your weight to the front of the board.

3. Now you are sliding the nose over the curb. Push your back foot out so your deck is at a right angle to the curb. You can help the slide by pushing with your front foot and leaning back on the slide a bit. This forces it along.

4. Exiting the trick can be done in a number of ways. The two most obvious are to lean back, taking the weight off the nose and onto the back kicktail, and literally dropping off. Or you can fakie by swinging the tail around and landing in much the same way.

This is a very good trick to learn because it can become part of a more complex move. You can do it frontside or backside, go in fakie, turn180 degrees and come off with a 180- or 360-degree rewind. If the ledge is higher than a curb, you can introduce flips.

Don't be fooled into thinking that tailslides are just as easy to learn as noseslides. This trick is definitely harder.

Technique

The hard part is landing the trick accurately because it is difficult to see as you land. When done backside, you are twisted away from the object and your weight naturally moves forward. Think of this trick as a 180-degree ollie and a noseslide.

1. As in the noseslide, pick a good ledge or rail and approach it from about the same angle. Ollie and shift your weight onto your trailing foot, pushing the tail onto the coping. The wheels will lock onto the coping and stop you from rolling back off the ramp.

2. Keep your weight on your back foot and slide it, pushing in a similar way to the noseslide.

3. To exit the trick in this instance, perform a small ollie to disengage the rear trucks and a 180-degree roll-off and keep riding in the direction you are going (normal). Alternatively, you can drag the board around 180-degree to land it fakie, which is much more impressive. The trick is harder to land fakie but easier to exit. The choice is yours!

②

③

This is a cool move in which you land on a rail or coping and slide along its length.

①

1. Approach the rail at about 30 degrees. As you get near the rail, ollie. It is crucial that you get good height with your ollie so you can be above the rail.

2. Now, this is the really tricky part. When you feel your deck is over the rail, bring the deck down by straightening your legs.

3. As with the other slides and grinds, push with your heels for a frontside slide, and for a backside slide, push the balls of your feet. On the backside slide, do not push too hard with your feet so you end up doing a face-plant.

Technique
This is not an easy trick because it takes skill and balance to execute properly. This trick is more dangerous than others because you will be sliding along hand rails, benches, or specially designed rails in skateparks.

4. When you get near the end of the rail or your momentum is falling to a point where you may stall, it's time to get off. If you are frontside, apply pressure to your back foot and turn the board through 90 degrees. Drop off and wait for the bromotion to start. One last bit of advice: when you learn this trick, start on low rails. You'll be grateful you did after falling off a few times!

When landed backside, this trick is much harder because you have to twist to land it and also twist to see where you are going.

CAUTION
This trick can cause serious damage if it goes wrong and may even cause your board to snap.

Pro Tips

- Hold your arms out for balance — one in front, one in the back.
- Slide with the deck at an angle, rather than dead center. If you put less stress on it, it is less likely to snap.

This is a great trick that can be used on a flat, on transitions between ramps, or just about anywhere.

Technique
This is one of the most popular tricks out there, so it's a must for your routine. Once you've mastered the ollie, nailing this should easy.

1. The start of this trick is almost the same as an ollie, but notice the feet are in slightly different positions. The main change is that the front foot is more to the edge of the deck than for a basic ollie.

2. Start in the same way as you would an ollie. As you do this, drag your front foot up the deck. As it reaches the kick, drag it. This pushes the board into a spin.

3. Once your board has rotated, it's time to stop it. Use your back foot to catch the board so that it stops rotating, and then stamp it back to the ground with your front foot.

4. As you land this trick, both feet and weight should be spread evenly — legs bent to absorb the impact and roll away.

Pro Tips

Here are a few pointers to help you nail this trick:

- First, make sure you perform this trick high enough to get the full rotation in, or you may land on the rail.
- Second — and this may be stating the obvious — make sure both feet are clear of the deck, or it won't spin. It will look as if you are doing a star jump because both of your feet shoot off in different directions. So, if you think star jump when you do the basic ollie, you are more than halfway there.

This trick is very similar to the kickflip and uses the same techniques as that trick and the ollie. But unlike the kickflip, this trick spins the opposite way.

Technique

Don't be tempted to put the book down and try this trick right away! Read on to learn important tips on how to become a radical heelflip master.

1. The start of this trick is the same as an ollie. Some people go wrong here by imitating the stance of the kickflip.

2. Jump as you would for an ollie. But as you drag your foot up, move it over to the other side of your deck and nose.

3. This is a fluid motion that should cause your board to rotate and level out. Catch the deck with your back foot, stamp it back to the ground, and roll away. Do not try to flip your board with your front foot over to the other side of your deck. When you jump, you'll just fall off!

Bigspin? Yes, You Can!

Now, it's time to get a bit more technical with your tricks.

Technique
This is basically a 180-degree backside with a 360-degree shuv-it mixed in for good measure. Timing and precise control are vital in achieving this trick.

1. Position your feet with your back foot on the tail, nice and central, and your front foot as if you were going to do a kickflip.

2. Now smack that tail down and jump, ollie-style. The movement of the front foot will send the board spinning 360 degrees.

3. At the same time as the front foot movement, kick back with your rear foot, sending the board spinning. Now you are spinning 180 degrees as the board is doing a 360-degree shuv-it.

4. Now your front foot comes into play to stop the rotation. Keep your foot near the deck throughout the move. Once the 360-degree rotation is done, bring the front foot down.

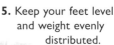

5. Keep your feet level and weight evenly distributed. Hammer the landing and roll away. Keep legs bent and your body loose throughout the move.

This may seem like a lot to take in, but it's easy if you break it down into individual elements. Try each bit separately before combining them to make it easier.

NOTE

Be sure not to do a pressure flip (having the ball of your back foot dead center). A pressure flip is a whole different animal. Your front foot should be doing the spinning bit, shuv-it style, not your tail kick, pressure-style.

This is the place where you can pull it all together and really show the world what you have learned.

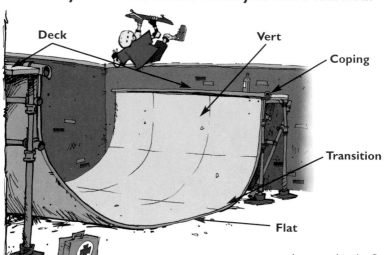

Deck — Vert — Coping — Transition — Flat

The Ramp

Before you start hitting massive airs, you will first have to get the feel of the ramp (see above) because it's like nothing you will have skated before. Put all your armor on and you're ready. It's best to start on a mini, which is like a vert but smaller, so that when you make a mistake you won't fall so far.

Technique

First, skate up to the transition, keeping your legs bent. As you hit it, relax your front leg and push with your back foot. This pump action will get you higher and speed you up. As you start to stall at the steep vert section, shift your weight to the back foot. If your weight is on your front foot too much as you hit the flat, you will stack. This delicate shifting of weight will come naturally after a while. When you feel confident, throw in a 180 or more at the stalling stage of your move. After a while, start to pump it. Get more speed up and try doing moves fakie. Most important, practice, get confident, and keep it all smooth and relaxed.

the deck. The next thing you do seems to go against what your body wants, but think of that stall feeling, and let your body drop over the edge.

3. Keep your weight forward and feet set, front foot snug in the bit before the tail kicks. Be warned: If you lean back at all at this point, you'll be served and your board will disappear over the top of the vert.

Stalling

This basic trick will start you off. Then it's just a matter of time before you grind and throw in some 180's, 360's, hand-plants and more. By now, you should have pumped your way to the coping, and thought, "Now what?" This is where stalling comes in.

1. As you reach the top of the vert, put pressure on the nose. This will cause the deck to rise at 90 degrees to the vert and the wheels to lock against the coping. You may rise with the board from the momentum. Stay cool. Gravity will now do its work and pull you back down. Take time to get used to this feeling.

2. Drop-ins are next, so saddle up and get ready for the drop. Put your armor on and place your board so that the tail is on

Backside Air

With air, it's best to start small, so come up the ramp at a slight angle. Stay compressed or you'll never reach your deck. As your front wheels clear the coping, start to reach down. When your back wheels and tail hit the coping, apply pressure to the tail, forcing the board into your hand. Kickturn off. Guide your body round (with your back foot). Stay compressed and you should, with the gentle arc, sail in, using gravity to make sweet contact with the vert again. Extend your legs and ride it out.

Backside 50–50 on Transition

Get up to the rail regular. Let your front wheels clear the coping (1) then, as your back wheels hit the coping, turn (2). This locks your wheels and back truck. When this feels good, stomp the front down. Grind it out to exit. Get your weight on the back kicktail and kickturn down the ramp (3).

360° Air

Once you feel safe about basic air, go big. Speed is needed to get the height required. As you leave the comfort of the ramp, twist your arm (only one as the other is holding your deck) and body. Whilst soaring like an eagle you can make that grab frontside, backside or mute – no more vanilla now.

Acid Drop

A little old school, but still a great way of getting speed out of the ramp from the outset, this looks cool. Practise on the flat first. Jump up as high as you can, keeping your feet level. As you reach to the top of your jump, place your board under your feet and let go of it. Straighten your legs and land. When you feel confident, do this move off the deck of a vert.

Blunt

Approach the coping with enough speed to clear the ramp and land with your back truck on the coping. Stall here as long as you can. Do an ollie or hand lift to exit the trick and go down the ramp.

Rock 'n' Roll

This is a good trick. As you approach the coping, shift your weight forward so your front truck clears the coping. Now rock on the middle of your board. On the way back from your rock, apply pressure to your tail and do a kickturn out. Land the front wheels and ride it out. Be sure to leave enough deck above the coping or you'll never make the kick as the front wheels will jam on the coping.

Boneless

This is an old-school trick that can be used on the vert, mellow bowls or even for street moves. As you go up a ramp and you are near the stalling point of the carve, step off with your front foot. Keep your back foot on the deck and, using the kick, raise the nose. Grab this with your hand. With your plated foot, kick off. This will launch you into a mellow, arcing air. Now let go of the board and bring your launching leg back onto the deck. Extend your legs for landing and roll away.

Hand Plants

This is another old-school move, but still looks great. Get some good speed up and shoot off the top of the ramp, holding your deck. For this, you must be in a squat position. As the momentum takes you up, extend one arm and hold the coping (think one-arm handstand). As gravity takes hold, turn and roll as if performing a cartwheel and bring the board back onto the vert. Ride it out.

Hand plant

Boneless

Keeping your skateboard clean and doing occasional maintenance will keep you on your feet and make your skateboard last that much longer.

Costs

The good thing about skateboarding is that, compared with other sports, maintenance costs are relatively low. You also need only a few tools to overhaul your skateboard. The main items you will need for a full service are pictured here.

Work Practice

Keep all the pieces you take off in order, clean them methodically, and reassemble carefully. Take a good look at everything: Check the deck for cracks, and check trucks and bushings for wear or cracks. Replace if necessary. You do not want to be pulling a

huge air only to see your truck fly off into the distance just before you get served big style.

It may seem like a pain to undo all the wheel bolts and rotate the wheels, but a rotated wheel will last much longer than one that isn't.

While your wheels are off, take out and clean the bearings. (See photos on facing page.) Use a toothbrush to get dust and dirt off, and, depending on type, strip them down.

Bearings can be non-serviceable (NS) or fully serviceable (FS). For NS bearings, only a brushing and wipe-down are required. A little more time and care are needed with FS bearings. First, clean off the outer grime, Then pop the "C" retaining clip and take off the protective shield, exposing the bearing. Brush out the grime, then soak the bearings in a cleaner. After five minutes or so, remove them. Let dry, and add a few drops of lubricant. Replace the shield snap in the "C" clip, add a bit of lubricant on the outside, and reassemble the bearings in the wheel. Easy!

Skate Sense

- Do not skate in wet conditions to protect your bearings. Rust will result, and your wheels will lock.
- Try not to skate through mud, gravel, and sand because these will get into and wreck the bearings.
- Use serviceable bearings; they last longer, saving you money.
- Be vigilant about tightening the bolts in your wheels. But do not overtighten, or you may squash the bearing case.
- If all-day sessioning is your style, carry a few spare parts and tools to enable you to service your board during the day. Nothing will wreck your session faster than a loose wheel and no wrench.

When you start putting together a custom board, your first one will be a mess. The deck may snap, the wheels will wear down to the bearings, the trucks grind down to the axle, and the balls go from your bearings.

Custom Boards

There are so many decks, trucks, wheels, and bearings to choose from, it would be pointless to suggest one or two. The pro skaters have their own labels; if these appeal to you, buy them. If you want to use the same setup as skateboarding legend Tony Hawk, go ahead – but it won't necessarily make you a better skater.

Most of the skateboards sold today are double-kicktailed, slightly concave and shaped like a bandage. In the past few years, longboards have started to make a comeback. Some people are also riding them on ramps, but they are mainly used for street carving and transport. Typically, they have wide trucks and large-diameter, soft wheels for comfort. The longboards come in a variety of shapes, such as pintails and swallowtails.

Kicktail

Truck

Spanner

Creating Your Own Skateboard

Some have cut-away wheel sections, some have kicks, others none.

Trucks

If you liked your first ones but don't want them again, talk to other skaters to see how well their trucks held out. It's a fact that they are strong and do not break that often, so you are unlikely to buy a really bad pair.

Wheels

If you like street, then your wheels should be slightly softer (94A) and larger (54 to 58 mm) than if you want to ride vert and parks (100A and 48 to 54 mm).

Bearings

There are many to choose from. They all have an ABC rating from 1 to 7. Seven is best, and the standards are not all based on just spinning. Whichever ones you choose, you're going to need eight altogether.

Below is a photograph of a skateboard and its components. So why not put together your own design?

Griptape

Deck

Nose

Wheel

Bearings

Acid Drop A large fall or gap that you typically jump into or over.

Airtime Leaving the ground.

Ally oop Basically, turning one way and spinning another, usually while catching air on a ramp.

Armor Protective pads and guards.

Backside grind Grinding anything with your back facing the rail.

Bacon in the pan Crashing and sliding down the ramp, then shriveling up like some frying bacon.

Banana See Goofy foot.

Banger Impressive trick.

Bromotion Skating in slow-motion.

Butter A trick that is pulled (or landed) really smoothly.

Carving Skating in a smooth arc, like surfing.

Chud Rough, uneven pavement.

Cooked A board that's been skated to annihilation.

Coping Metal railings on top of a vert ramp.

Deck or blank The bit you stand on.

Deck diggler Someone who dangles his board near the coping.

Dropping in Entering a ramp from the top.

Exit How you come out of a trick.

Face-plant To injure yourself.

Fakie Anything (approach, exit, trick or spin) done backward.

50–50 Grinding both trucks equally.

Fluid or Butter Smooth and flowing well-executed trick.

Frontside Anything executed with body facing ramp or obstacle.

Fruit booter An in-line skater.

Fun box A box for doing stuff on.

Goofy foot Leading with your right foot.

Grinding Sliding or grinding parts of deck or truck over anything.

Grip tape Rough sandpaper-type material used for grip on your deck.

Grommet (Grom) Novice skater.

Halfpipe U-shaped ramp.

Hammering Nailing or landing a trick well.

Hardcore Skaters not afraid to take risks.

Jack To hit yourself on something.

Lid Helmet.

Melting Coming up really fast to a trick, then just fizzling out.

Mints Small wheels.

Mute a type of grab.

Nollie An ollie,

but done with
the nose.

Nose Front
of deck.

Oil check
Falling over.

Okie Not so sharp.

Ollie Basic trick in
which you make the
board hop.

Pads See Armor.

Pop Doing a trick.

Perp Streetlurker,
pedestrian.

Pros Professional
skaters.

Rail Coping.

Regular Riding with left
foot forward.

Rewind Spinning off a
rail the opposite way
you spun on.

Road rash Cuts and
grazes from falling over.

Scrape Inexperienced
person on rental
equipment.

Session Time spent
skating.

Served Someone who
eats it big time.

Shuv-it Using your feet
to move the board
along.

Sketchy A trick that
was not landed well.

Skid-lid Helmet.

Slammed
Fell over
while skating.

Spore Novice
skater.

Street iron Stair
rails and similar
objects used for
grinding while
skating in public places

Stunt dubz Someone
who does the same
trick right after
someone else just to
show she can do it.

Transition Part of
ramp that takes you
from vertical to
horizontal.

Trouter Someone
who brags all day.

Trucks The bits that
keep the wheels on
the deck.

Tweak Pain caused
by getting served.

Twiddler A skater who
lands oddly and then
readjusts his feet.

Vanilla No thrills.

Vert U-shaped ramp.

Wacker A real
potato head.

What Now?

So you've done it. At first you thought it impossible, but you've learned to perform some real bangers. Whether you're a mellow-carving longboarder or vert hammerer, you'll earn maximum respect as you sledge your way around the park. But where do you get more info? Here are a few ideas to keep you up on the latest in tricks, new parks and breaking news.

Magazines

Bookstores may have hard-to-get magazines from around the world. These often carry breakdowns of new moves and skater profiles.

Internet

Just type "skateboarding" into the search engine and you're off. Or type in names of specific tricks. You may even be able to track down skateboard companies so you can even e-mail them to get advice.

Skateparks

Your local skatepark owner may put on events or arrange skateboarding competitions. Money raised from these events may be used to improve the park, so get involved.